Math Counts

Children's Press®

An Imprint of Scholastic Inc.

About This Series

In keeping with the major goals of the National Council of Teachers of Mathematics, children will become mathematical problem solvers, learn to communicate mathematically, and learn to reason mathematically by using the series Math Counts.

Pattern, Shape, and *Size* may be investigated first—in any sequence.

Sorting, Counting, and *Numbers* may be used next, followed by *Time, Length, Weight,* and *Capacity.*

—Ramona G. Choos, Professor of Mathematics,
Senior Adviser to the Dean of Continuing Education, Chicago State University;
Sponsor for Chicago Elementary Teachers' Mathematics Club

Author's Note

Mathematics is a part of a child's world. It is not only interpreting numbers or mastering tricks of addition or multiplication. Mathematics is about ideas. These ideas have been developed to explain particular qualities such as size, weight, and height, as well as relationships and comparisons. Yet all too often the important part that an understanding of mathematics will play in a child's development is forgotten or ignored.

Most adults can solve simple mathematical tasks without the need for counters, beads, or fingers. Young children find such abstractions almost impossible to master. They need to see, talk, touch, and experiment.

The photographs and text in these books have been chosen to encourage talk about topics that are essentially mathematical. By talking, the young reader can explore some of the central concepts that support mathematics. It is on an understanding of these concepts that a student's future mastery of mathematics will be built.

—Henry Pluckrose

Math Counts

By Henry Pluckrose

Mathematics Consultant: Ramona G. Choos, Professor of Mathematics

Children's Press®

An Imprint of Scholastic Inc.

Weight is a measuring word. We weigh things to find out how heavy they are.

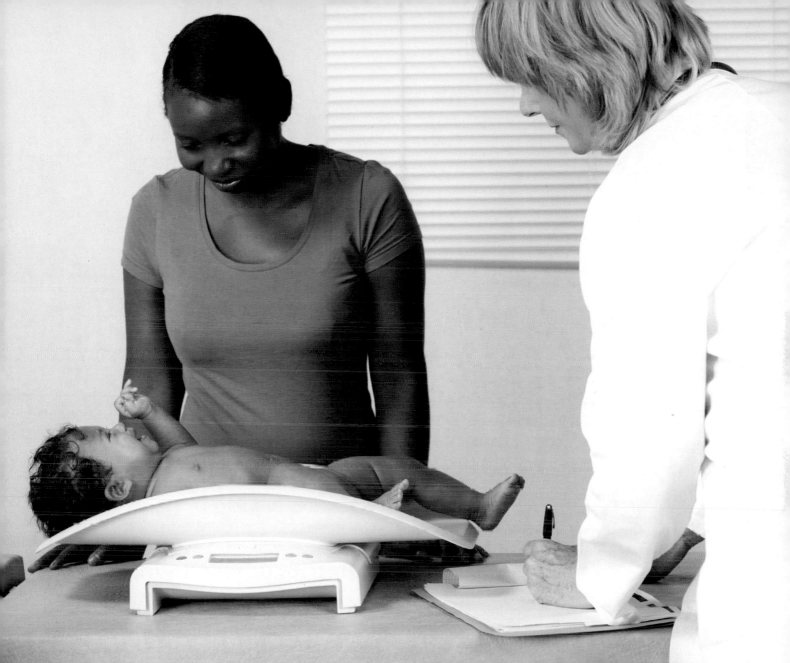

Why do we need to measure weight?
Doctors check the weight of babies
to make sure they are growing properly.

5

We weigh ingredients when we cook. Only a small quantity of flour is needed to make a cake. We weigh small quantities in ounces or grams.

The flour is being weighed before it is sent to the bakery. Large quantities of flour are needed to make all the bread sold in a supermarket. Large quantities are weighed in pounds or kilograms.

Everything weighs something, even very light things like letters or postcards.

There are lots of letters and postcards in these mailbags. Why are the bags so heavy?

Sometimes we can guess the weight of things.
Which do you think is lighter, the feather or the stone?

How would you make sure that you have guessed correctly?

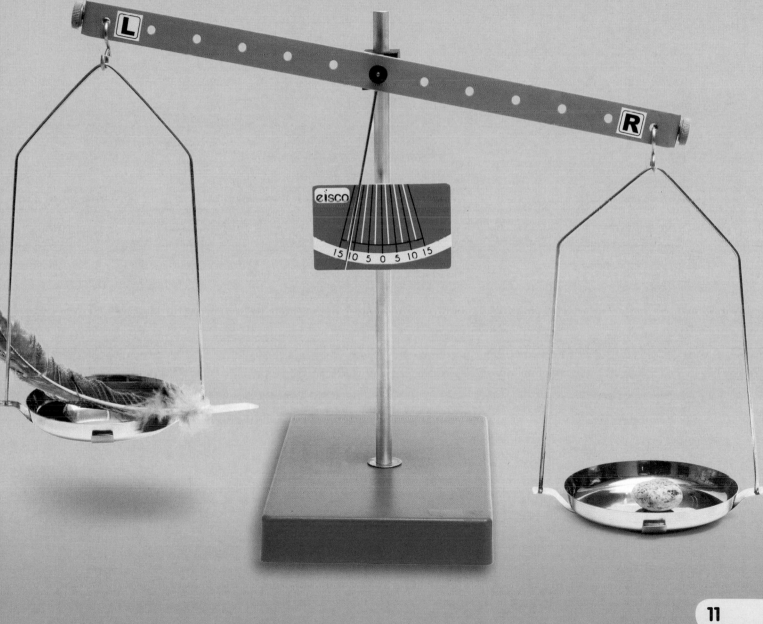

Guessing that one thing is heavier than another is not always easy.

How will you find out for sure
which pile of tea is heavier?

You could put a stone in one pan of the scale.
Which is heavier—the teabags

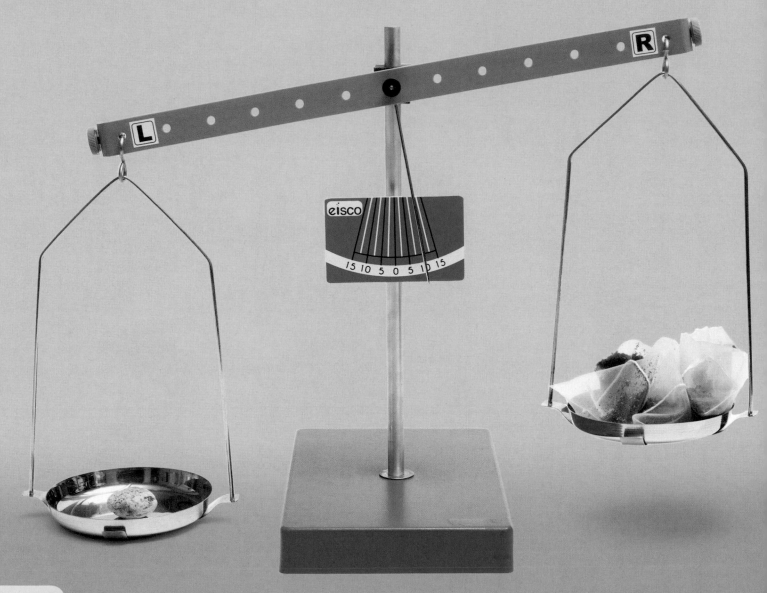

or the tea?
How do you know?

But stones come in different weights.
So standard weights are used to measure heaviness.
We use ounces and pounds. 16 ounces equal 1 pound.
Many countries use grams and kilograms.
1000 grams make 1 kilogram.

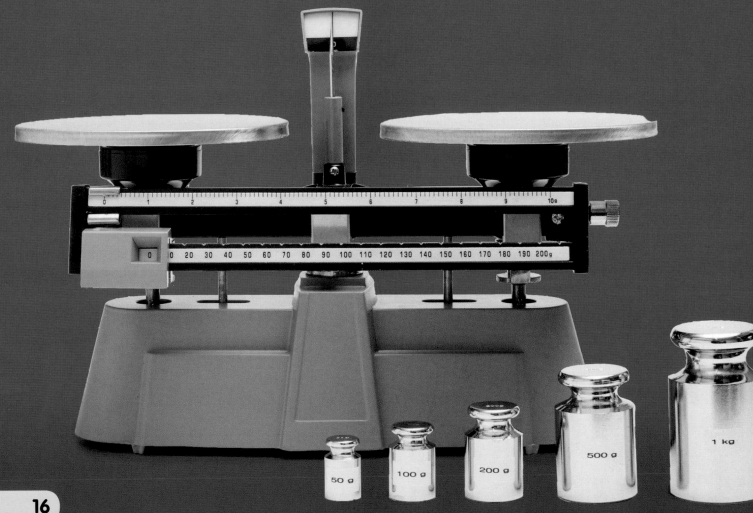

A kilogram of apples weighs
exactly the same wherever you buy it.

If the apples were heavier than a kilogram,
the scales would not balance.

If the apples were lighter than a kilogram, the scales would not balance either.

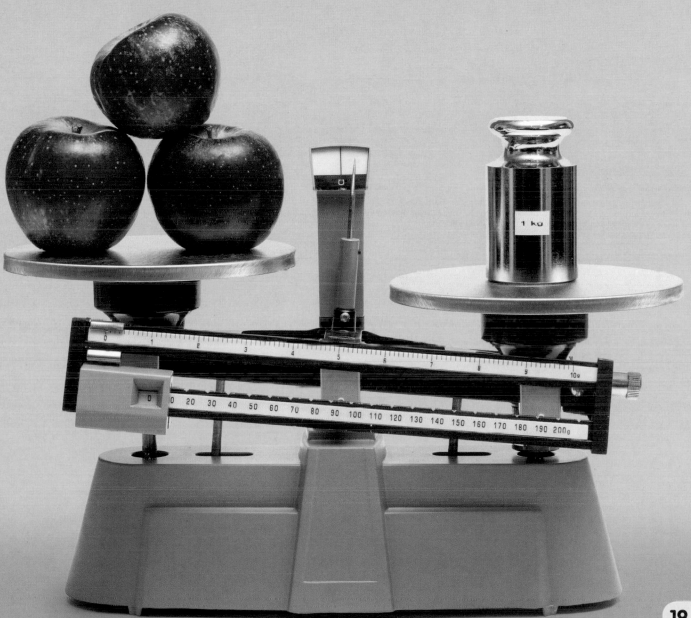

You can use scales to compare the weights of different things. A kilogram of apples is as heavy as a kilogram of potatoes.

Would a kilogram of rice weigh more than, less than, or the same as a kilogram of cheese?

It is important to know how heavy things are. Clerks often weigh food when they sell it. We pay for the weight of food that we buy.

Even when food is sold in packages, the weight of the contents is marked on the label.

Exclusively sourced from our MEDITERRANEAN PRESERVE

La

SEA + SALT

Fine

THIS SALT DOES NOT SUPPLY IODIDE A NECESSARY NUTRIENT

NET WT. 26.5 OZ. (1LB., 10.5 OZ.) 750g

MILK FROM GRASS-FED COWS

PURE IRISH BUTTER

Net Wt. 8 OZ (227g)

BAKING
Double Acting
POWDER

NET WT 8.1 OZ (230g)

FUEL

SKIPPY

NET WT 16.3 OZ (1 LB 0.3 OZ) 462g

GO

Ca
A

NETWT
PESO NETO
15.5 OZ (439g)

PRIME

Protein
Power

CHOB

GREEK

NON-FAT
YOGURT

NET WT
5.3 OZ (150g)

Whole Wheat
Crackers

Baked with 100%
Whole Grain

NET WT. 7 OZ (200g)

BEE COMPANY

tupelo
HONEY

NET WT.
340g /12oz

1869
TOMATO
KETCHUP
57 VARIETIES

GROWN NOT MADE

NET WT 20 OZ (1 LB 4 OZ) 567g

ECCO

86

Rigatoni no. 24

ni no. 24

Al dente
12 min

DO DE CECCO

NAL RECIPE FOR OVER 130 YEARS
MADE IN ITALY

1 lb (453 g)

IBLE BEE

Light Tuna

NET WT 5 OZ (142g)
DR WT 4 OZ (113g)

Luggage is weighed at the airport before it is loaded onto a plane.

If the plane were overloaded,
it could not fly safely.

Trucks and vans must not be overloaded either.
This small truck could not carry

something as heavy as this.

A crane operator
has to be sure that
the crane is strong enough
to lift the weight
of the goods it is moving.

Signs next to some bridges tell drivers
the weight that each bridge can support.
Very heavy trucks cannot travel over this bridge.
The bridge would not hold their weight.

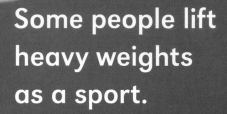

Some people lift heavy weights as a sport.

How heavy were you when you were last weighed? Are you heavier now?

Index

Reader's Guide

Visit this Scholastic Web site to download the Reader's Guide for this series:
www.factsfornow.scholastic.com Enter the keywords **Math Counts**

Library of Congress Cataloging-in-Publication Data
Names: Pluckrose, Henry, 1931- author. | Choos, Ramona G., consultant.
Title: Weight / by Henry Pluckrose; mathematics consultant: Ramona G. Choos,
Professor of Mathematics.
Other titles: Math counts.
Description: Updated edition. | New York, NY: Children's Press, an imprint of Scholastic Inc., [2018] | Series: Math counts | Includes index.
Identifiers: LCCN 2017061282| ISBN 9780531175156 (library binding) | ISBN 9780531135242 (pbk.)
Subjects: LCSH: Weights and measures—Juvenile literature.
Classification: LCC QC90.6 .P58 2018 | DDC 530.8—dc23
LC record available at https://lccn.loc.gov/2017061282

Copyright © The Watts Publishing Group, 2018
Printed in Heshan, China 62

Scholastic Inc., 557 Broadway, New York, NY 10012.

1 2 3 4 5 6 7 8 9 10 R 28 27 26 25 24 23 22 21 20 19

Credits: Photos ©: cover letters: boykung/Shutterstock; cover gold bars: Pixfiction/Shutterstock; 1 letters: boykung/Shutterstock; 1 gold bars: Pixfiction/Shutterstock; 3 gold bars: Pixfiction/Shutterstock; 3 letters: boykung/Shutterstock; 4: Gary John Norman/Getty Images; 5: lostinbins/iStockphoto; 6: Emely/Cultura/ZUMAPRESS.com/Newscom; 7: Breedfoto/Shutterstock; 8: Panther Media GmbH/Alamy Images; 9: Scott Olson/Getty Images; 10: Bianca Alexis Photography; 11: Bianca Alexis Photography; 12: Bianca Alexis Photography; 13: Bianca Alexis Photography; 14: Bianca Alexis Photography; 15: Bianca Alexis Photography; 16: Bianca Alexis Photography; 17: Bianca Alexis Photography; 18: Bianca Alexis Photography; 19: Bianca Alexis Photography; 20: Bianca Alexis Photography; 21: Bianca Alexis Photography; 22: Blend Images - Tanya Constantine/Getty Images; 23: Bianca Alexis Photography; 24: LightField Studios/Shutterstock; 25: Asergieiev/iStockphoto; 26: Art Konovalov/Shutterstock; 27: DarthArt/iStockphoto; 28: Zabavna/Shutterstock; 29: Alex McGregor/Alamy Images; 30: Matthias Hangst/Getty Images; 31: Tetra Images/Getty Images.